The Century's Best Book of Poetry

Written by Sasha Brown
A.K.A: Misha, J. Williams, Caran, Roshacka

I0107916

DISCLAIMER: This is a work of fiction. Unless otherwise indicated, all the names, characters, businesses, places, events and incidents in this book are either the product of the author's imagination or used in a fictitious manner. Any resemblance to actual persons, living or dead, or actual events is purely coincidental.

Copyright © 2021 Sasha Brown

All rights reserved. No part of this publication may be reproduced, distributed, or transmitted in any form or by any means, including photocopying, recording, or other electronic or mechanical methods, without the prior written permission of the author, except in the case of brief quotations embodied in critical reviews and certain other noncommercial uses permitted by copyright law. For permission requests, contact the publisher at:

www.Holon.co

ISBN#: 978-1-955342-05-6 (Paperback)
ISBN#: 978-1-955342-39-1 (eBook)

Published by:

Holon Publishing & Collective Press
A Storytelling Company
www.Holon.co

Contents

THE CENTURY'S BEST BOOK OF POETRY

Sasha Brown
Jeanne Bregman
Caran Bregman
Misha
Roshacka

December 13, 2020
School of Life and Love and Heartbreak

MY DREAM

The young lady walks
She sees, she listens
She feels her feet step on the cement
Of the parking garage in the year 2040
She listens to the sound echo through the walls
She steps to her hovercraft and listens
to another sound
Of echoing feet
As Susanne swipes her hand over the lock and raises
the door, a deep male voice
"Stop right there"
The young woman reaches deep into her black purse
and pulls out a small gun.
"This is it," she thinks – a moment too late to stop —
The only sound she heard was her boyfriend
screaming, "NO it's ..." and the boom of the pistol.

LIFE EXPLOSION

When this life explodes
And mortar hits hard
When he said he loved her
And it was all a lie
When she cried out in pain
"Not Now!!"
When we think we have it made
Then life is shredded
To bits and pieces
When he heard she had
Screamed
In pain and agony
He laughed at her pain
Laughed at her
anger
She looked at him
All she could say
"Why?"

SPEED IS EVERYTHING – *by Sashtiger1*

Rockin and Rollin
Down the Road
Signs flash by
Lights trail
The world flies by
With amazing
SPEED!
We rock
We roll
We rock and roll
Down the road
Pass them
By
A rocket
Speeding to the moon
Rockin and rollin
Kicking back in space
A world or two
Apart
Unknown
This is my dream
As I fly

SPIRIT LIFE

Here we stand
For all to see
Light Shining
Luminosity
Illuminating
The Faces
Of death
Becoming life for
All to live
Joy at eternal life
Fear of working at the camp
Thoughts come and go
While the reality passes
Slowly by
Fright with the pain
Eternal damnation
From where we came
As we go now
Where life ebbs
Slowly away
Or eternal salvation
Which it will be
For you and I
As we cross the road
Together as we
Our spirit taking our place
Not carefully do they rise
Nor do they need to be
As all who can see them
is of their kind
Floating away
Into nothingness
That is not nothing

FOR YOU

Here I stand
Alone I am not
Here I am
Here I wait
I am here
      For you
I am here
      To be with you
I will always
      Be here
For You

FIGHT

Fight for your right
To love
To live
For happiness
Fight for your right
To speak
To stand up for yourself
To be with whom you want
And always remember to
Fight for your right
To be who you are
                          Yourself!

MY SOUL FEELS

My soul
Feeling so much
My soul
Feeling your love
My soul
Feeling your happiness
My soul
Feeling your anger
My soul
Feeling all you feel

HERE I AM

So here I am
Sitting thinking
Of you
So here I am
Sitting
With only you
On my mind
And in my heart
So here I am
Sitting
Waiting
Loving
And
Thinking only of you — I am here

DIFFERENT – *a diversity song written first in 1991*

I see you standing there
     Waiting for me
I feel your presence
     Right beside me
I feel your heart
You feel my heart
     Chorus: It doesn't matter if we are different –
it is our ongoing love forever, love forever. Love forever...
If society claims
     We can't be together
Then society should change
If you are of a different race
We can still be together
No matter what society says
     Chorus: It doesn't matter if we are different –
it is our ongoing love forever, love forever, love forever...

LIFETIMES

As the moon
Rises over
The sun
And the
Stars act
Like the suns rays
So will you rise
Over any other
Person I know
When early
Morning sun
Begins to rise
Over blue
Mountains
So will we shine
In a bright
And sunny way
And when
The night
Comes again
My only
Hope is when
The moon rises
Over the sun
And night comes
Still we will
Be here
Together
For ever

A MYSTERY

This life is a mystery —
It just passes by
All I can do is ask why
My life is a joy
          Although pain passes by
          And I still cry
My image stands true
          Though all can see through
          This shell of me after you
I lay alone — not me after all
          Because though you're with me
          You're not here when I call
After you, I am not who I was
          Long ago when we fell in love so true
And before I became so blue
Now I lay under stars so bright
Alone in the world — dreams out of sight
I play in grass so green waiting to be seen

THE BLACK SKY

The black sky
Full of rain bearing clouds
Looms dark and heavy over us
Thunder booms
Out over the earth
The animals startle and
Begin to run
The wall of rain
Moves through the valley
Leaving destruction
Behind it
Fallen trees and floating dog houses
Speed down the river
The people watch with
Utter amazement as everything
They
Worked for Is washed away

A TREE

A lady under a tree
Watching — waiting
For the storm on the horizon
To come in
She will have to go under shelter
A man watching the planes
At the airport
Knowing soon he will
Be on the other side of the world
Leaving behind all he comprehends
Me, looking out a window
And now knowing what is there
And being there all the same
All have one thing in common
Making changes for the better
To achieve a state of near perfection

TRUST

We can't keep our hands away
We only hope this time we will stay
We fold our hands and pray
We will understand each other
We will listen to one another
We won't hide behind a cover
Give trust to another
We will say all of our hopes and fears
Through all the laugher and
The happiness and fears and the tears
Bridge: Through the years the happiness and the tears
Chorus: we will work it out(x3)

POWER

Round and round
The merry go round
Going nowhere
But do we care
The horses go up
The horses go down
The horses are flying
Falling to the ground
We watch the rain fall
Day by day
Running from the sky
To tease and torment
Us
As we go
We rise
With power and speed
We fight
The world
With raging eyes
Power and greed
Supercede all
Other ideals
We must make
It real
Take it over
Start again
On different levels of
Power and
Stability

THE NIGHT FELL

The night was still
A quiet calm
As darkness settled
Across the land
Like a shroud
Their screams were
Heard — loud — awakening
The silent land
And caused a rumble
Silenced with a heavy hand
They watched with patience
The storm roll in
Covered their eyes
When the lightning came
A gentle hand
Came down
And stopped the rain
They looked up
To see shining stars
And a moon so bright
It shimmered off the cars
And a sound of relief
Swept through the crowd
As silence again settled across the land

UPS AND DOWNS

My life is full of
Ups and downs
I feel so low
I might tumble to the depths
Of the earth
And when I am high
I might fly
Off the earth
And reach the moon
And be lost
I might die
And see nothing
But the blazing fires of hell
I will live
And see myself live
And then dig
With bleeding fingers
My grave

MEAN NOTHING

The things I see
The things I hear
Mean nothing
The rocks
In the earth
Dig in to my feet
As I run but
Mean nothing
The wailing siren
Of the police car
Roaring past me
Means nothing
The punks I see
The music I hear
Everything I do
Means nothing
As I hide
From myself

NOTHING LEFT

If there is nothing left
Is there anything to gain?
Madness
Swirling
Whirling
Twirling
Spinning
Through my
Mind
As a
Tornado
Rips apart
The land
Gaining power
Momentum to
Rip
The continent
In half — like my mind

CRAZY

How long does it take to reach insanity?
Is it just a step across a line
Or many steps — to reach a common goal
Is the society right?
Or its refugees
Must we fight
To achieve peace
Do we never agree
Just to live in happiness
Or must I leave
An adventure unknown
Alone
Does it matter
What I need
It does not
Does it matter
What I want
It does not
Does having cloth matter
With no one to sew it together?
Do relationships matter
With no depth behind them?
Must I be a token
Added only when needed
I do not wish the routine
I do wish meaning something
I do wish variety
And I wish to pursue
Mental growth and
Change throughout my life
Through diversity

TO UNDERSTAND

Do you understand
Do you want to
Does one step
Push you over
The edge
Able to hang on
To nothing
Unwanting
Not needing
Nothing mattering

LOST

Trying to be lost
In a world of thoughts
Not knowing
Not caring
What happens next
Does my world
Come crashing down
Like thunder in the sky
Trying so hard
To be lost in
A world of thoughts
Will anything
Get better
As time flies
Through our cries
Of pain
And anguish
The lightning strikes
And changes
Our world
Is it better
Or
Is it worse
We know not now
But will soon know
Did it work
Or crash?

LIFE

Life is a mystery
To you and I
That plays games
Behind the clouds
In the sky
Life is a mystery
To you and I
That hides itself
Behind the tears
In our eyes
Life is a mystery
To you and I
That passes by
With a word
A wing
 A prayer
Life is a mystery
That passes by — it never lies

WHEN

When my thoughts run away
When I am here to stay
When I'm feeling blue
Or tell all that's true
When something's not right
When it's out of my sight
When I looked inside
And started to cry
When it makes me mad
Or I feel sad
When I feel it
In my bones and
I start to jones
When I am glad
Instead of sad
When I look
Before I leap
I don't have to count sheep
Before I go to sleep
I know I'm doing well
When I think
About what I do
I'll mess up
But not as bad
But when I do
This time
I won't be sad
This time
I'll be alright

WHIPLASH

He was here
And now he's gone
What do I do
With a life that's
Been thrown
For a curve
Around the world
Whipping by
Time to fly
With the wind
Blowing around my ears
The fire
Ripping apart my flesh

PAIN

When does the pain fade away
Of dreams shattered
And thoughts denied
When do new patterns mold
To replace outdated ones
Scattered across the plains
And set free to become new
When do the tears stop falling
How do you feel new
Like a spring breeze
How do you feel happy
Like a bucking colt
How can you feel free
A bird on the wind

FREE TO DREAM

What in the hell
Do I have to do
To work my way out
Of this mess I'm into
My life deals me this
When I know not
When I am confused
About my territory
When I will be free
What can I do
To be freer than
A bird
To fly
In the sky
And dream the dreams
Of the free

ALL AROUND ME

All around me
People talk
People listen
People study
People watch
All around me
People look
People feel
People cry
People angered
All around me
People with
So many things
In their minds
As I silently look
All around me

NEVER FORGET

Never Forget
        To live for
        Yourself
        Not for others
Never Forget
        To love yourself
        And your human
        Family
Never Forget
        To brush
        Your teeth
Never Forget
        To breathe
        In and out
        Every day
And most of all
        Never Forget
        That I love you

Sasha Brown

I Think of You

I think of you
The way you smell
The way you breathe
The way you
Talk to me
I think of you
The way your
Lips touch mine
A sweet, loving
Kiss
I think of you
The way you hold me
And comfort me
When I am down
I think of you
My heart lifts
My eyes glimmer
When I think of you

CHOICES

I see my future
An empty glass
Waiting to be filled
I can fill it
With anything
With hatred, anger and
Forcing pain on others
I can fill it
With love, happiness and
Making life better for all
There are choices to be made
I choose what is
Right for me
Everything I do
Will come back to me
What shall I choose?

A Tiger

A tiger
Laying in wait
For the prey
A tiger
Waiting
For its kill
A tiger
Ready
For almost anything
I am
A tiger
I am
Waiting
I am
Ready

CHANGE

As sorrow
Fills my heart
Tears pour down
My face
In a flood
Of pain
As I look
Behind myself
At life
How I alone
Have put myself
Through hell
As I look
Forward
I tell myself
To step ahead
Change
Do better

NEVER-ENDING L

My life will never dissipate
Because of my love for you
I love you so much
I have only heard your voice
You seem so brilliant
Like the moon and stars at night
Your mind so bright
The way you look
Means nothing
The way I feel
Nothing could stop me
I feel so high
When I talk to you
My love for you
Is
Never ending

MY HEART

My heart
Filled with love
For you
My heart
Before you
Only blue
My heart
Before you
So cold
My heart
With you
I'll never grow old
My heart
Eternity and
A day
My heart
Don't break it
I pray

BONUS: THE SOLDIER INSIDE

I looked down at my bloody body in disbelief. I looked small, and next to his body — what was left of it — I looked even smaller. I had to figure out how we got this way. I looked down at myself, and my spirit body shimmered in the sunlight coming through the window. I remembered then, the sunlight triggering a memory of our arguing. Our fights had started out bad enough and had only gotten worse over time, but I had wanted to give him a chance because I had promised him his temper would never get in the way of my love for him. I was proud that I had kept my promise, but apparently the rosy ending I had wanted my life to turn out like had not been destined for me.

How *had* I gotten here anyway, a spirit looking over my body from a perch in my room? It began several years ago.

Xander and I had just gotten together, about six months prior, when he took me to a hotel, a nice place, and I was excited about going to a hotel with him for the first time. When we got there I wanted to take a shower and look pretty for him, and I got out of the shower perky and bouncy and looked forward to the evening ahead. A deep voice that did not sound like Xander said from a dark corner,

"What did you do?"

I could only stutter, my mind reeling. This looked like Xander, but as he stood up it clearly couldn't be *my* Xander. This deep-voiced person carried himself in a different way, sounded different, yet had the features of my Xander. Who was this guy that could be my boyfriends' twin?

"Huh?" I managed to get out.

"Do not get smart with me. Who is he?" Xander-not-*my*-Xander said, and threw something past my head. "The fool you are hanging out with when you are not with me!"

"There is no one!"

"Liar! Misha how could you do this to me?"

All of a sudden he came after me, hitting me in the side of my head so hard I lost my balance, falling on the bed before realizing what a weak position I had placed myself in. There was no escape as he hit me over and over again in my head, boxing my ears and beating my body, taking care not to hit me where bruises would show. All the while Xander was screaming in this voice not his own, like he was possessed by a demon.

Eventually he got tired of screaming questions at me that I had no answer to, and finally, not getting the responses he was looking for, he fell asleep on the bed next to me. The next morning he asked if I had been beat up by someone while he was asleep and that I looked like hell. I told him if he couldn't remember I was not going to remind him, and we went on our way home. I also had woken with a terrible buzzing sound in my head — like wasps or mosquitoes — that never went away.

Several months went by with no major events, so when he asked me to marry him I happily said yes. During the time we were preparing for the wedding, Xander came up to me and said,

"We need to talk."

I was positive he was going to break up with me, but instead he sat me down and told me he had a temper, "A bad one," in his words. He talked at length about the time he had spent in the military, and that he suffered from a brain injury and Post Traumatic Stress Disorder (PTSD). He said it affected his moods, and that he couldn't always really control it, but that he was trying. I asked some questions, and asked if his temper was related to when people did things that were bad, like cheating on him or lying to him. He said it was, and I promised then and there that I would never leave him due to his temper, and that we would not have that problem that he had with his exes; because I am neither a cheater or a liar, and therefore the temper would be unnecessary, and we would be fine. He insisted I think about it before I made such a promise, and I said,

"I do not need to think about it. I do not cheat and I do not lie, so you won't need to have a temper at all with me in the same way. I won't be provoking it like the rest did."

"Don't say you weren't warned," was the unsettling response I received.

My mother lived in Las Vegas, and we decided that even though her religion would probably mean she would not come to our wedding, we would get married there, 500 miles away from our hometown, in order to give her the chance to come. She lived in an assisted living center there, so we got ready, booked our wedding chapel, and left for Las Vegas.

While we were away, Xander brought up the fact that he had kept his temper under control for quite awhile, and I of course told him I was proud of him, but on the inside that made me a little nervous. We went to see my mom, and as predicted she advised us that she could not attend the wedding which was not in a Catholic church, and that was the only way she could attend. We were not about to change the chapel we had booked, and I promised I would come see her on my wedding day to show her my dress and have a cup of coffee with her — our traditional way of celebrating for many years. She agreed that would be great and seemed happy as we drove away.

We got married the next day after doing a hurried shopping expedition for Xander's wedding outfit. We had a beautiful ceremony, and I brought Xander back to our hotel and told him I would return shortly with dinner. I went, showed my mom my dress I was still in, placed an order at a local restaurant we enjoyed, and went to their carside pickup spot to get our wedding night dinner. I brought it back to our hotel and enjoyed a nice dinner with my Xander. We went to the slot floor and played a little while before Xander wanted to go back upstairs. I stayed to play for a few more minutes, yet bored quickly and followed him up. As soon as I got to the room I knew something was wrong. It was not my Xander that greeted me, but the other one, the not-so-nice one. I was in utter disbelief that of all nights, it was on my wedding night the other Xander came to play. How could this possibly be? My thoughts raced through my head going over what I had done so wrong as to bring him out. I really couldn't fathom that being away from me for only 10 minutes could do this.

Out of the darkened room, I heard the other Xander's voice, "You...Cheated...on...me!"

My heart sank to the basement of the 20 story hotel as I realized what he was thinking. "What? No!" I said. "I went to see mom, I got dinner, and I came right back here! And tonight I was only on the casino floor for a few minutes... How could you think I would do that to you anyways?"

He obviously didn't believe me and slapped me across my face so hard I stumbled. I ran into the bathroom and took a shower praying the entire time my Xander would be there when I got out. Luckily he was, and we had a peaceful night thereafter. As time went on, however, we began fighting more and more, and things took a bad turn to where I was actually physically defending myself. Eventually, one day, it happened where I actually got hurt and hurt him too. We had been arguing, and he was going into his room and I tried to stop him, and somehow my hand got caught in the doorjamb between it and the door. Well, just like in a cartoon, (it makes me laugh to think of the picture now) my hand was flattened pretty much like a pancake with the meat hanging off in strips. Also, when I pushed the door open as he pulled it open I was screaming and I pushed it too hard, and broke two of his fingers. That day he swore I must have hurt myself at work, and that I was just making up the whole thing. I went to school and tried to forget, but it was bothering me and I approached Xander a few days later and said,

"Xander, we gotta chill out or one of these days one of us is gonna wind up dead, and I am not honestly sure which one." I really am in total love with Xander, and I can't possibly ask for a better man, because in between everything life is fantastic. We have a good life... well we did...before we wound up bleeding out on our floor, together that is... and I looked over at my Xander. My Xander! Oh its spirit Xander! And he would be crying if he could be, if he had a body. And I know I would be if I could be, and he floats over to me *(floats? I am not used to not having a body yet, will I ever be?)* And he is telling me he is sorry and I am telling him I am sorry; I never meant it to end this way, and we realize we are earthbound. Dear Lord what now? God only knows.

The End Or The Beginning

www.ingramcontent.com/pod-product-compliance
Lightning Source LLC
Chambersburg PA
CBHW051740040426
42447CB00008B/1230

* 9 7 8 1 9 5 5 3 4 2 0 5 6 *